CUTE & EASY Pirates & Cowboys! CAKE TOPPERS

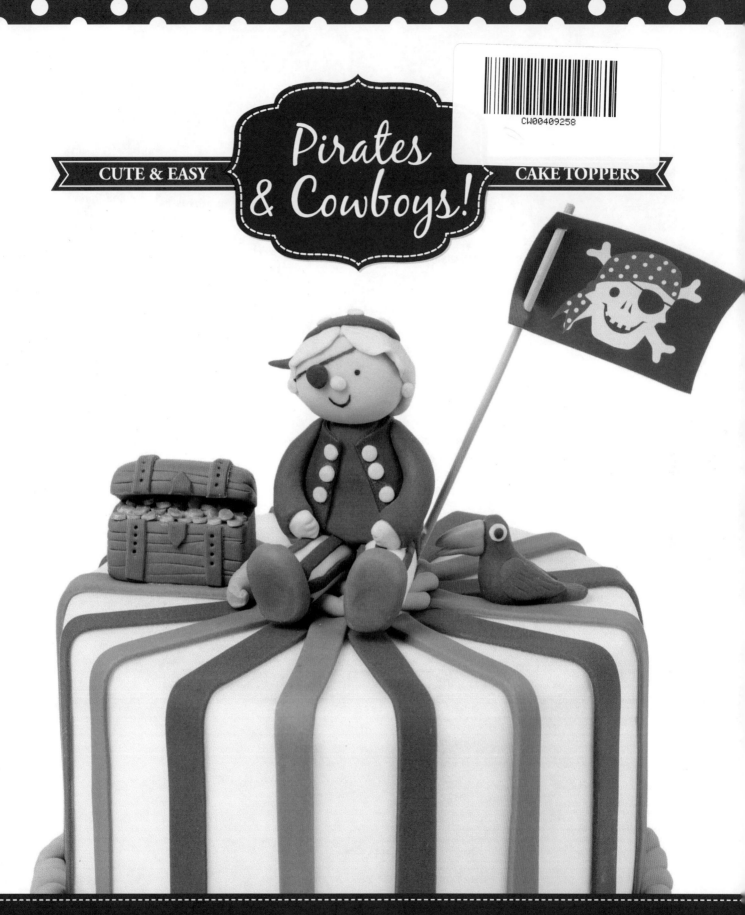

Cute & Easy Cake Toppers
for any Pirate Party or Cowboy Celebration!

Contributors

Following a career in finance, Amanda Mumbray launched her cake business in 2010 and has gone from strength to strength, delighting customers with her unique bespoke creations and winning several Gold medals at various International Cake Shows. Amanda's **Clever Little Cupcake** company is based near Manchester, UK:
www.cleverlittlecupcake.co.uk

Amanda Mumbray

Helen Penman has been designing cakes for over 15 years and her work has been featured in a wide range of cake books and magazines. She has also written several cake decorating and modelling books of her own, and runs a successful cake company from her home in Kent, UK
www.toonicetoslice.co.uk

Helen Penman

Lesley Grainger has been imaginative since birth and has baked since she was old enough to hold a spatula. When life-saving surgery prompted a radical rethink, Lesley left a successful corporate career to pursue her passion for cake making. Lesley is based in Greenock, Scotland. Say 'hello' at:
www.lesleybakescakes.co.uk

Lesley Grainger

First published in 2014 by Kyle Craig Publishing

Text and illustration copyright © 2014 Kyle Craig Publishing

Editor: Alison McNicol

Design and illustration: Julie Anson

ISBN: 978-1-908-707-56-7

A CIP record for this book is available from the British Library.

A Kyle Craig Publication

www.kyle-craig.com

Contents

Welcome!

Welcome to **'Pirates & Cowboys!'**, the latest title in the **Cute & Easy Cake Toppers** Collection.

Each book in the series focuses on a specific theme, and this book contains a gorgeous selection of beautiful cake toppers perfect for any pirate party or cowboy celebration!

Whether you're an absolute beginner or an accomplished cake decorator, these projects are suitable for all skill levels, and we're sure that you will have as much fun making them as we did!

Enjoy!

Fondant/Sugarpaste/Gumpaste

Fondant/Sugarpaste – Ready-made fondant, also called ready to roll icing, is widely available in a selection of fantastic colours. Most regular cake decorators find it cheaper to buy a larger quantity in white and mix their own colours using colouring pastes or gels. Fondant is used to cover entire cakes, and as a base to make modelling paste for modelling and figures (see below).

Modelling Paste – Used throughout this book. Firm but pliable and dries faster and harder than fondant/sugarpaste. When making models, fondant can be too soft so we add CMC/Tylose powder to thicken it.

Florist Paste/Gumpaste –The large and small shoes in this book are made using florist paste as it is more pliable than fondant, but dries very quickly and becomes quite hard, so it is widely used for items like flowers that are delicate but need to hold their shape when dry.

Florist Paste can be bought ready made, or you can make at home by adding Gum-Tex/Gum Tragacanth to regular fondant.

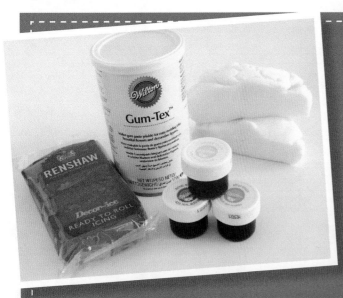

How to Make Modelling Paste

Throughout this book we refer to 'paste', meaning modelling paste. You can convert regular shop-bought fondant into modelling paste by adding CMC/Tylose powder, which is a thickening agent.

Add approx 1 tsp of CMC/Tylose powder to 225g (8oz) of fondant/sugarpaste. Knead well and leave in an airtight freezer bag for a couple of hours.

Add too much and it will crack. If this happens, add in a little shortening (white vegetable fat) to make it pliable again.

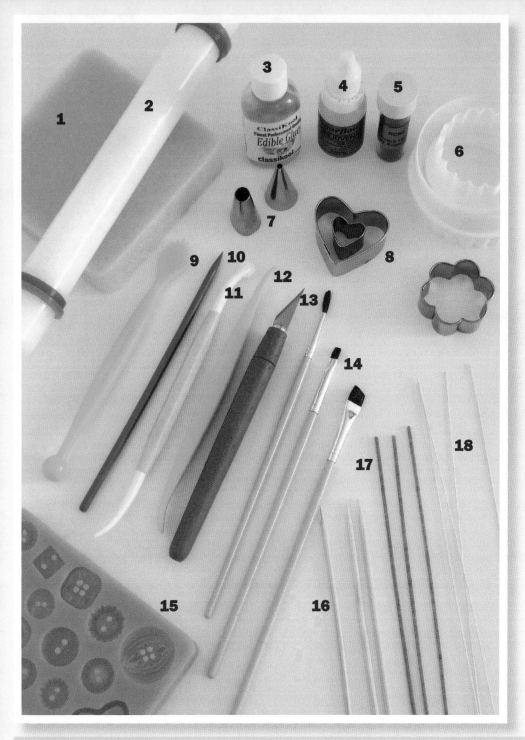

1 Foam Pad – holds pieces in place while drying.

2 Rolling pin – acrylic works better than wooden when working with fondant/paste.

3 Edible glue – essential when creating models. See below.

4 Rejuvenator spirit – mix with food colourings to create an edible paint.

5 Petal Dust, pink – for adding a 'blush' effect to cheeks.

6 Round and scalloped cutters – a modelling essential.

7 Piping nozzles – used to shape mouths and indents.

8 Shaped cutters – various uses.

9 Ball tool/serrated tool – another modelling essential.

10 Small pointed tool – used to create details like nostrils and holes.

11 Quilting tool – creates a stitched effect.

12 Veining tool – for adding details to flowers and models.

13 Craft knife/scalpel – everyday essential.

14 Brushes – to add finer details to faces.

15 Moulds – create detailed paste buttons, fairy wings and lots more.

16 Wooden skewers – to support larger models.

17 Spaghetti strands – also used for support.

18 Coated craft wire – often used in flower making.

Edible Glue

Whenever we refer to 'glue' in this book, we of course mean 'edible glue'. You can buy bottles of edible glue, which is strong and great for holding larger models together. You can also use a light brushing of water, some royal icing, or make your own edible glue by dissolving ¼ teaspoon tylose powder in 2 tablespoons warm water. Leave until dissolved and stir until smooth. This will keep for up to a week in the refrigerator.

Little Cowboy

1 Let's start with the cactus plant! Roll out a sausage of green paste.

2 Insert a bamboo skewer into the sausage.

3 Roll out another two sausages, cutting off each end at an angle.

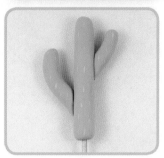

4 Attach the arms of the cactus and paint the prickles with white food colouring. Set aside to dry.

5 Roll out a cylinder of paste, insert a toothpick through the centre and, using a veining tool, mark the trouser details.

6 Roll out a cylinder of light blue paste for the body and gently place over the toothpick.

7 Roll out a smooth ball for the head, and place on top of the body, snipping the toothpick with some scissors if it is too long.

8 For the hat roll a small ball of paste, flattening the top with a paintbrush handle to create a ridge through the centre.

9 Place the shape over a piece of rolled out paste, and cut a circle all the way around it then turn up the edges of the brim.

10 Add a little strip to conceal the join, and a little star. Leave to dry for a few hours before placing on the head.

11 Add a strip of brown paste for the belt. Use two square cutters, one slightly larger than the other to make the buckle.

12 Cut a triangle of paste and arrange around the neck. Place a little star on his chest.

13 Use a pastry circle for the hair. Cut away a section to create a parting and mark with veining tool. Add eyes, and dust cheeks with petal dust.

14 Add the hat, securing with a little glue.

Little Cowgirl

Materials

Modelling paste:
Egg Yellow
Flesh
Dark Brown
Pink
Paprika
Food colouring: white
Edible pen: black
Petal dust: pink
Edible glue

Tools

Craft knife/scalpel
Veining tool
Toothpick
Pastry circles
Small star cutter
Fine paintbrush

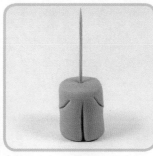

1 Roll out a cylinder of pink paste. Insert a toothpick through the centre and, using a veining tool, mark the trouser detail

2 Roll another cylinder of paste for the body and place on top of the legs.

3 Roll out a smooth ball for the head.

4 Add a darker strip for the belt.

5 Add a little star for the belt buckle.

6 Cut out two teardrop shapes for the waistcoat and attach with glue.

7 Cut out a triangle of paste and arrange around the neck.

8 Use a pastry circle to make a circle for the hair, cutting a small section for the parting. Add the hair detail using the veining tool.

9 Add two small teardrop shapes for the bunches, and two tiny little balls for the hair bobbles.

10 Roll out a ball of paste and flatten the top with a paintbrush handle.

11 Place the shape on top of some rolled out paste, and cut out a circle all around it.

12 Use a toothpick to make the brim slightly upturned.

13 Add a strip of paste to conceal the join, and add a little star. Leave to dry for a few hours.

14 Secure the hat with glue. Draw on her eyes, add blush with petal dust, and add some polka dots and stitching details.

Little Horsey

1 Roll out four small sausages and insert toothpicks into each one. Leave to dry for a few hours.

2 Roll out a long sausage shape for the body.

3 Insert the legs into the body.

4 Add a little ball of paste to attach the head to.

5 Roll out a pear shaped piece of paste for the head. Press down near the middle to create a dip in the face shape.

6 Attach it to the body.

7 Using a pastry circle, cut out a contrasting piece of paste for the nose. Mark the nostrils with the end of a paintbrush. Support the head with a little foam.

8 Add a flattened white teardrop shape to the forehead.

9 For the tail, roll out a tapered sausage, and using small scissors snip into it.

10 Make a hole at the back of horse, and insert and glue in the tail. Also add a little sausage of paste at the back of the head to attach the mane.

11 Roll out lots of little sausages for the mane and glue to the strip down the back of the neck.

12 To make the saddle, cut out a piece of paste in a figure of eight shape and mark around the edges with the quilting tool.

13 Mark the mouth with the back end of a piping nozzle. Add a few strips of paste to make the reins and bridle.

14 Mark the eyes with an edible marker pen. Add in a dot of white edible paint for the pupil.

Little Cowboy Cupcakes

Materials

Modelling paste:
Egg Yellow
Dark Brown
Red
Baby Blue
Black
Food colouring: white
Edible pen: black
Petal dust: silver
Rejuvenator spirit
Edible glue

Tools

Craft knife/scalpel
Quilting tool
Veining tool
Star cutters: large & small
Pastry circle cutters
Toothpicks
Fine paintbrush

1 First cut some plain topper discs – one per cupcake – and set aside to dry.

2 Roll out a long sausage of paste.

3 Fold the sausage in half and twist it together.

4 Arrange into a lasso shape.

5 Attach to a disc of sugar-paste.

6 Every cowboy needs a hat!

7 Roll out a ball of paste and flatten the top with a paint-brush handle.

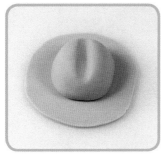

8 Place the shape on top of some rolled out paste of the same colour, and cut out a circle all around it.

9 Use a toothpick to make the brim slightly upturned.

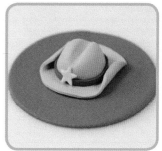

10 Add a strip of paste to conceal the join, and add a little star. Attach to a disc of sugarpaste.

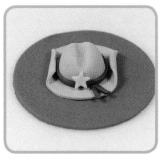

11 Roll out two tiny sausages, and attach to the brim.

12 This birthday cake is going with a bang!!

13 Roll out a long red sausage and cut into four equal lengths.

14 Cut two strips of black paste and attach as shown. Make little holes in the top of each sausage with the end of a toothpick.

15 Roll out a very fine sausage of black paste and cut off four small pieces. Leave them to dry for a few minutes, so they are easier to insert into the holes.

16 Attach to a disc of sugarpaste and add a few little stars.

17 Watch out, the Sheriff is in town!

18 Cut out a large star shape.

19 Attach the star to a disc of sugarpaste.

20 Add five tiny balls to the tip of each point of the star, flattening slightly.

21 Write the word sheriff – or the child's name! – on with edible pen.

22 A lucky birthday horseshoe!

23 Cut out a tapered strip, making it fatter in the middle.

24 Bend into a horseshoe shape, trimming off the ends if necessary.

25 Attach to a disc of sugarpaste and mark the detail with a veining tool.

26 Paint the horseshoe with a little silver lustre.

27 Cute cowboy neckerchief!

28 Cut out an elongated triangle shape as pictured.

29 Attach a little ball of paste to a disc of sugarpaste.

30 Wrap the triangle shape around the ball and secure both ends together.

31 Paint on some detail with food colouring mixed with rejuvenator spirit.

32 Time to take the bull by the horns!

33 Roll out a sausage shape, tapering at both ends.

34 Bend both ends up into a horns shape.

35 Cut out a rectangle shape of paste, using the quilting tool to add a bit of extra detail.

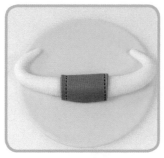

36 Attach the horns to a disc of sugarpaste, and secure the strip over the centre.

37 What a cute little horsey!

38 Roll out a pear shaped piece of paste to make the head.

39 Using the smallest pastry circle, cut a mouth area from light brown paste. Mark the nostrils and mouth as per the horsey on the previous page.

40 Add a flattened teardrop shape across the top of the head and down the front of the face.

41 Attach the head to a disc of sugarpaste, adding a few tiny sausages for the mane. Draw on the eyes using an edible pen.

42 A cactus you can eat!

43 Roll out a sausage and trim at the base.

44 Roll out a further two sausages and cut both ends at an angle.

45 Attach and arrange the cactus on a disc of sugarpaste.

46 Paint on the prickles with a fine paintbrush and food colouring.

Materials

Modelling paste:
White
Egg Yellow
Dark Brown
Light Brown
Red
Petal dust: brown
Edible glue

Tools

Craft knife/scalpel
Large star cutter
Cel stick
Fine paintbrush

1 Start by preparing your cake, covering in white sugarpaste/fondant.

2 Roll out some brown modelling paste and, using a knife, cut out random shapes and attach to the sides of your cake.

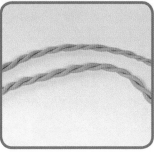

3 Roll two sausages and twist them together.

4 Arrange them around the base of the cake, gluing in place.

5 For the main body of the hat, using just paste make a large ball and flatten it with the palm of your hand.

6 Using the side of your hand, indent the top. If your hat is larger, you could also mould this shape from rice krispie treats and cover with paste.

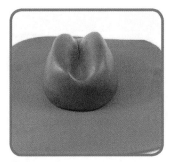

7 Place the shape over a piece of rolled out paste, securing with some edible glue.

8 Using a craft knife, cut all the way around the hat to create the brim.

9 Using the cel stick, roll the brim upwards.

10 Add a strip of paste to conceal the join.

11 Roll two sausages together and attach to the brim.

12 Cut out a large star and attach to the front of the hat.

13 Roll out five tiny balls of paste, and attach to the points of the star.

14 Once dry, brush with a little brown petal dust to make it look worn and position on top of cake.

Cute Cowboy

Materials

Modelling paste:
Royal Blue, Sky Blue
Flesh, Red
Egg Yellow
Dark & Light Brown
Black, White
Edible pen: brown
Edible paint: white
Petal dust: pink
Edible glue

Tools

Craft knife/scalpel
Dresden tool
Veining tool
Small star cutter
Small number cutter
Small circle cutter

1 Trace the Cute Cowboy template from the rear of the book using greaseproof paper or baking parchment.

2 Roll a thin layer of sky blue paste and cut a 7" to 8" circle from it (to fit your cake size). A side plate is often the perfect size for this!

3 Roll a thin layer of flesh coloured paste and lay the template on top. Mark the outline of the face, including the ears, with a veining tool.

4 Follow the indented outline and use a scalpel to cut the shape. Don't glue any of the pieces to your topper until all are complete.

5 Roll a thin layer of brown paste and lay the template on top. Mark the outline of the COMPLETE cowboy hat and cut either in one or two pieces.

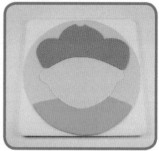

6 Repeat Step 5 to create the shoulder area.

7 Repeat Step 5 to create the neckerchief.

8 Finally, repeat Step 5 to create the hair.

9 Create eyes by rolling two equal size balls of paste and pressing flat. Add a little white dot with a tiny ball of paste.

10 To create a nose, roll a small ball of flesh coloured paste and slightly flatten.

11 Add a mouth and eyebrows with edible pen or by rolling very thin sausages of paste.

12 Give your cowboy a rosy glow by dusting the cheeks with petal dust. Add a little to the inner ears too.

13 You can also add details to the neckerchief with edible pens/paints or simply by adding dots of coloured paste.

14 Personalise by adding a sheriff's badge and add the child's age. Glue all cut pieces to your topper disc, allow to dry then place on cake.

Materials

Modelling paste:
White, Black
Royal Blue, Sky Blue
Red, Egg yellow
Dark & Light brown
Flesh
Edible pens: green, brown
Edible paint: white, silver
Edible glue

Tools

Craft knife/scalpel
Veining tool
Quilting tool
Round cutter, 68mm (2¾")
FMM geometrical cutter set
Selection of small star cutters
Small number cutters
Small blossom/daisy cutter
Small paintbrush

1 First, cut one 68mm (2¾") topper disc for each cupcake planned. Set aside to dry. Now, cut a piece of tan paste using the mid-size oval cutter.

2 Use your largest round cutter to cut into the oval piece to create the hat brim.

3 Cut another piece with the mid-size oval cutter. Use large round cutter to cut just over half way down, then the smallest oval cutter to cut a notch from the top of hat crown.

4 Add a narrow strip of black paste.

5 Assemble both pieces on your cupcake disc. Add a yellow star to complete your design.

6 Trace the cactus template from the rear of this book.

7 Roll a thin piece of pale green paste and, using your veining tool, transfer the outline of your template.

8 Use your scalpel tool to cut the cactus shape.

9 Place on your cupcake disc, trimming the excess from the bottom and add detail using your green edible ink pen.

10 Add cactus flowers using a tiny blossom cutter if you wish.

11 Cut a star from thinly rolled yellow paste.

12 Use a smaller cutter to create an indent inside this shape.

13 Use your veining tool to create a little detail around the edges.

14 Roll five small balls of yellow paste and press to flatten. Attach to the points of the badge.

15 Cut a small circle of yellow paste, indenting with a smaller cutter if you wish. Add the child's age in a contrasting colour.

16 Trace the cowboy boot template from the rear of the book.

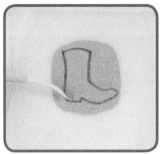

17 Roll a thin piece of brown paste and, using your veining tool, transfer the outline of your template.

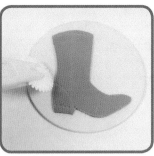

18 Use your scalpel tool to cut the cowboy boot shape and then your stitching tool to add detail.

19 Cut two small pointed strips of dark paste and glue to the boot.

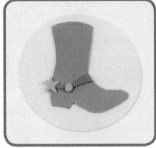

20 Add a tiny, flat ball of paste and star in grey. Paint these details silver to add a little style!

21 Cut a circle of grey paste.

22 Cut a smaller circle from the inside (slightly up from the centre) and create a cut at the top.

23 Pull slightly to elongate and trim at the ends to form a horseshoe shape.

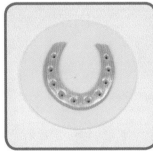

24 Use your veining tool to add detail and paint silver if you wish.

25 Create two long, thin sausages of beige/tan coloured paste.

26 Twist both lengths together.

27 Arrange on your cupcake disc in a lasso shape.

28 Roll a thin piece of red paste and cut into a square.

29 Fold the square over, leaving a slight overlap.

30 Attach to your cupcake disc in a neckerchief shape.

31 Decorate the neckerchief with small white painted details.
.

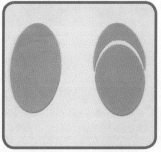

32 Cut an oval of thinly rolled dark brown paste. Trim part way down using your oval cutter (to fit cupcake disc).

33 Cut an oval of thinly rolled light brown paste. Trim part way down with a round cutter to create the horse's muzzle.

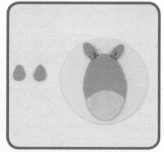

34 Make two teardrops of tan paste. Pinch in the centre to create ears and trim to fit.

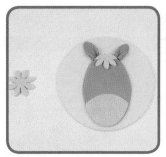

35 Cut a small daisy of beige paste and trim to fit.

36 Cut a strip of thin red paste. Lay across the muzzle and trim to fit.

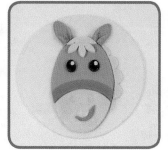

37 Add eyes (tiny ovals of dark paste), nostrils (indent with ball tool), a mouth (tiny sausage of tan paste) and a mane (edge trimmed from fluted circle cutout).

38 Cut thinly rolled dark brown paste using the smallest oval cutter. Use the cutter again to split this into pieces as shown.

39 Cut another oval and split, as shown. Use the side of your cutter across the centre and the tip at the top.

40 Cut thinly rolled flesh coloured paste using the mid-size round cutter. Then cut with the side of your oval cutter to fit this piece with the cowboy hat.

41 Create shoulders by cutting a circle then cut a further circle from the centre.

42 Remove the centre circle and lay the remaining piece on your cupcake disc. Trim shoulders with your scalpel tool, as shown (right).

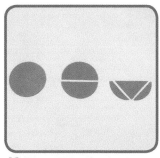

43 Cut a circle of red paste (mid-size round cutter), split this in half then cut a triangle from one of the semi-circles.

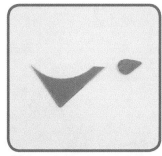

44 Trim the neckerchief to fit with your round mid-size cutter. Add a little red teardrop shape to the side.

45 Add eyes (tiny balls of black paste), a nose (ball of flesh paste) and draw hair and mouth with edible pen. Add a yellow star to the hat.

46 Complete by adding little white painted details.

Materials

Modelling paste:
Red
Black
Flesh
White
Buttercream
Edible paint: white
Edible glue

Tools

Craft knife/scalpel
Rolling pin
Veining tool
Round cutters: various sizes
Pizza wheel

1 Start with a dome-shaped cake, and cover with buttercream. Cover with smoothly rolled flesh paste and smooth to finish.

2 Roll and cut a large circle from red paste (a large cake board makes a good template). Cut in half, glue to cake, smooth and trim.

3 Cut several spots from white paste and glue to headband.

4 With more flesh paste, shape a nose and ears as shown. Mark the mouth using a large circle cutter.

5 Shape a tassel and knot for the cap, as shown, and glue to one side of headband.

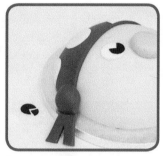

6 For the eye, cut a medium white circle and a smaller black circle, cutting a ¼ of the black circle away. Glue in place.

7 Make the eye patch from a long, flat strip of black paste, plus a thick black circle.

8 Secure the patch on top of the strap over where the eye would be, glue in place and trim off excess.

9 Prepare each cupcake by adding buttercream then cut and add a disc of flesh paste, smoothing into a dome shape.

10 Mark the mouth with the end of a piping tube, add a nose and ear, and one little eye with a dot of black paste.

11 Roll thinly and cut out a large circle of red paste. Cut in half and glue to the top of the cupcake.

12 Take a small ball of black paste, flatten, and glue the little eye patch in place.

13 Cut out a strap for the eye patch, attach to the cupcake as shown.

14 Cut out a strap for the eye patch, attach to the cupcake as shown.

Materials

Modelling paste:
Red
White
Flesh
Black
Dark & Light Brown
Yellow
Green edible wafer paper
Edible glue

Tools

Craft knife/scalpel
Veining tool
Toothpicks
Bamboo skewer
Green floristry wire (20 gauge)
Circle cutters: various sizes
Square cutters
Lily cutters
Fine paintbrush

1 Let's start with the palm tree! Roll out a sausage shape, tapered slightly.

2 Insert a bamboo skewer, and mark the bark detail with a veining tool.

3 Use a lily cutter to mark the shape of the palm leaves on the wafer paper. Cut them out and then cut a jagged shape into each leaf for a more realistic look.

4 Attach to the top of the tree using a little floristry wire. Leave to dry in a cake dummy. You can also use green paste for this, but allow to dry overnight before attaching.

5 Roll out a cylinder of paste and insert a toothpick through the centre. Mark the trouser detail with a veining tool.

6 Roll out another cylinder for the body.

7 Roll out a smooth ball for the head.

8 Cut out some fine strips and place horizontally around the body, gluing carefully in place.

9 Cut out another strip to make the belt, and use two small square cutters to make the buckle.

10 Cut a circle in half for the bandana, attach two small teardrop shapes to make the ties and a small ball to make the knot.

11 Add a little teardrop shape to make the kiss curl.

12 Draw on the eyes using the edible marker pen, and dust the cheeks using a little pink petal dust.

13 Make a sword by cutting out two strips of paste - one longer and angled at end and one shorter. Attach a small flattened ball for the handle.

14 Glue the sword to the side of the body.

Materials

Modelling paste:
Flesh
Sky blue
Light brown
Pale pink
Dark pink
Yellow
Edible pen: black
Edible paint: white
Petal dust: pink
Edible glue

Tools

Craft knife/scalpel
Veining tool
Tapered cone
Toothpick
Circle cutters: various sizes
Blossom cutters
Fine paintbrush

1 Roll out a cylinder of paste and insert a toothpick through the centre. Mark the leg detail with a veining tool.

2 Roll out another cylinder for the body.

3 Roll out a smooth ball for the head.

4 You can make the frilled skirt in two different ways. The first is to cut a long strip and frill with the tapered cone tool.

5 The second way to make the frills is to cut out two circles and frill one edge

6 Attach three layers of frills to the legs.

7 Add a strip for the waistband.

8 Add strips of paste for the hair, and a little blossom at her waistband.

9 Cut a circle in half to make the bandana, and two teardrop and a ball shape to make the tie at the side.

10 Mark the eyes with the edible marker pen, and dust her cheeks with a little pink petal dust. Paint on some white spots to her bandana.

11 For her sword, cut out a small strip, mark down the centre, and cut the end to make it pointed.

12 Attach a flattened ball for the handle.

13 Glue on a further strip under the handle to complete the sword.

14 Attach the sword to her side.

1 Start by cutting a disc of paste for each cupcake you are planning. Set aside to dry.

2 Make a tapered sausage shape for the trunk of the palm tree

3 Attach the sausage to a disc of sugarpaste and add on the bark detail with edible pen.

4 Cut out two palm tree leaves from green wafer paper. If you don't have this, use green paste and allow to dry.

5 Attach to the top of the tree with a tiny amount of edible glue – too much and the paper will disintigrate.

6 Time to hunt for buried treasure!

7 Cut out a map shape, as pictured, to fit on your topper disc.

8 Use the craft knife to cut away small notches around the edge.

9 Place on a disc of sugar-paste, and roll the edges up with your fingers.

10 Draw on the detail with edible marker pens.

11 Look! We found the treasure!

12 Roll out a sausage shape, and flatten at the bottom and both ends, leaving the top still rounded.

13 Using a veining tool, mark the detail for the lid.

14 Cut two strips of black for the straps, and mark the wood detail with a veining tool. Flatten a ball of paste for the lock. Use the end of a straw for the detail.

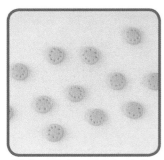

15 Cut out lots of little circles, pricking them around the edges using a cocktail stick.

16 Arrange everything on a disc of sugarpaste, and paint the lock and coins with gold lustre.

17 Can you say 'pretty polly pirate's parrot' very quickly ten times??

18 Roll out a sausage shape, tapering at one end, and indenting half way up.

19 Bend the head back on to the body.

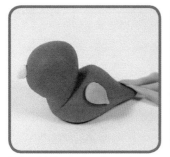

20 Add three teardrop shapes for the tail feathers, two teardrops for the wings, and a tiny ball of paste for the beak.

21 Place on a disc of sugarpaste, and draw on the eyes with an edible marker pen.

22 Every pirate needs a hat!

23 Roll out a small ball of black paste.

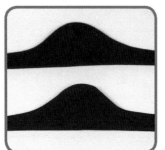

24 Roll more paste and cut out two humped shapes as pictured.

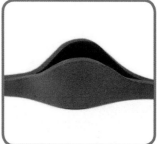

25 Arrange these shapes around the ball of paste to create the pirate hat.

26 Place on a disc of sugarpaste and paint on the skull and crossbones with white food colouring.

27 This little guy is having a whale of a time!

28 Roll out a ball of black paste, and taper at one end, bending it back on itself to create the tail. Make a hole in the top of the head with the end of a paintbrush.

29 Add a little heart for the tail fins, and three teardrop shapes for the water from the blow hole. Mark the mouth with the scallop tool.

30 Flatten a ball of paste for the eye, and draw the pupil on with an edible pen.

31 Attach the whale to a disc of sugarpaste.

32 Who is this nippy little guy?

33 Roll out four little sausages, and a ball of sugarpaste, and arrange them as pictured above.

34 Roll out two tapered sausages and cut the widest part in half.

35 Arrange the pincers around the front of the crab.

36 Mark the mouth with the scallop tool, and add two little balls for the eyes, drawing on the pupils with an edible pen.

37 Anyone for a sword fight?

38 Cut out a strip of paste, marking it down the centre. Use the craft knife to make the end pointed.

39 Add a flattened ball for the handle.

40 Attach a second strip to the handle.

41 Attach to a topper disc. You can also paint with gold lustre dust if you wish.

42 Message in a bottle!

43 Cut out a rectangle of paste.

44 Roll up the paste.

45 Make a tapered sausage and open up the neck of the bottle with a cone tool.

46 Attach to a disc of sugarpaste, and add a small rectangle to make the bottle's label. Draw on the detail with an edible pen.

Materials

Modelling paste:
Blue
Red
Black
White
Grey
Light & dark brown
Baking parchment
Edible glue

Tools

Craft knife/scalpel
Veining tool
Small skull & crossbones mould
Round cutters; various, small
Alphabet cutters

1 Trace the Pirate Ship template from the rear of the book, using greaseproof paper or baking parchment. Ensure you make a cake this size or larger.

2 Roll a thin layer of blue paste and cut a circle – the same size as your cake - from it using a cake board or plate as a template.

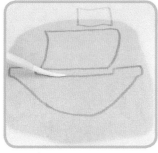

3 Roll a thin layer of light brown paste, lay the template on top and mark the outline of the boat hull using a veining tool.

4 Following the indented outline created by your veining tool, use a sharp scalpel tool to cut the shape.

5 From the same brown paste, cut a long, thin strip to create the mast.

6 Repeat Step 3 with red paste to create the mainsail.

7 Repeat Step 3 to create the black flag.

8 Loosely blend a few shades of blue to create a marbled effect. Use the same plate template as Step 2 to cut a semi-circle of marbled paste. Create 'waves' using a small round cutter.

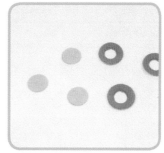

9 Cut some small circles of grey paste using two small round plunger cutters, cut a small circle of dark brown paste then a smaller circle from inside.

10 Lay on top of each other to create the portholes.

11 Cut small white circles to add to your mainsail. Glue in place.

12 Add a skull & crossbones to your flag (we've used a small silicone mould but you could paint one using edible white paint).

13 Cut child's name using alphabet cutters.

14 Assemble all and attach to the top of your cake.

1 Cut a paste topper disc for each cupcake you are making, set aside to dry. Trace the small pirate ship template (hull and sail) from the rear of the book.

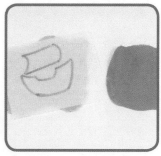

2 Lay the template on top of thinly rolled brown paste (hull) and red paste (sail) and use your veining tool to mark the outline.

3 Use your scalpel tool to cut out both pieces.

4 Cut a long thin strip of brown paste to create a mast and a tiny black flag for the top of the mast. Glue pieces to a topper disc.

5 Add detail to your design with edible ink pens and white edible paint (food colouring mixed with rejuvenator spirit).

6 Trace the treasure chest template from the rear of the book.

7 Lay the template on top of thinly rolled brown paste and mark the design with your veining tool.

8 Use your scalpel tool to cut out the treasure chest.

9 Add detail to your design with edible ink pens and edible gold/silver paints.

10 Add little circles and paint these gold to create some coins!

11 Trace the template of the pirate hat from the rear of the book.

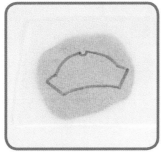

12 Lay the template on top of thinly rolled black paste and mark the design with your veining tool.

13 Use your scalpel tool to cut out the pirate hat.

14 Use a tiny silicone mould to add skull and crossbones detail....

15 ...or paint freehand with white edible paint if you're feeling artistic!

16 Cut a blue paste circle using your round cutter. Use the same cutter again to cut a sand coloured circle with piece removed, as shown.

17 Trace the palm tree template (trunk and branches) from the rear of the book.

18 Lay the template on top of thinly rolled brown paste (trunk) and green paste (branches) and use your veining tool to mark the outline.

19 Use your scalpel tool to cut out both parts.

20 Attach all pieces to your cupcake disc and add details with edible ink pens.

21 Trace the template of the skull and crossbones from the rear of the book.

22 Lay the skull and crossbones template on top of thinly rolled white paste, using your veining tool to mark the outline. Use your scalpel to cut both pieces.

23 As crossbones tips can be tricky to cut, use little heart shapes instead. Simply cut the points away, as shown...

24 ...and add to the ends of your crossbones – easy!

25 Assemble all pieces on your cupcake disc. Use tiny round cutters to create the eyes, your scalpel to cut the nose and teeth or draw all with edible pen.

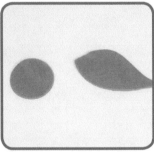

26 Cut a small circle and leaf from some thin red paste, as shown. Both should fit comfortably together on your cupcake disc.

27 Cut a small black heart and small black circle. Trim both to fit the body, creating a beak and feet.

28 Cut three small different sized leaf shapes in bright colours, overlap and add to the parrot's body.

29 Add a small circle of white paste with a little dot of black paste in the centre to create an eye.

30 Add little details to your parrot with white edible paint. You can also cut a little piece from the beak with your scalpel tool.

31 Cut a rectangle of dark beige paste.

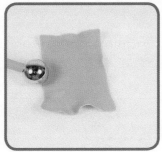

32 Using a ball tool, thin the edges all the way around.

33 Roll opposing corners of your treasure map, as shown.

34 Using edible ink pens, draw some cute directions on the scroll.

35 Cut a circle of flesh coloured paste slightly smaller than your topper disc.

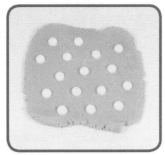

36 Create spotted paste by placing small white circles on top of pink paste....

37 ...then roll until the dots blend. Roll in opposing directions to prevent the dot shape distorting.

38 Cut the shape shown with a round cutter to create a bandana.

39 Cut two long leaf shapes to create hair. Trim any excess.

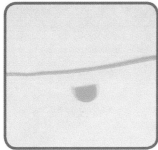

40 Create a pretty eye patch by cutting a long strip of pink paste and a little 'u' shape, as shown.

41 Add a little eye (ball of black paste) and nose (ball of flesh coloured paste).

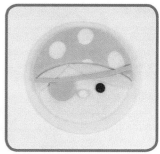

42 Attach the eye patch.

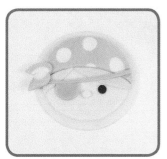

43 Create two tiny teardrops to form a bandana knot.

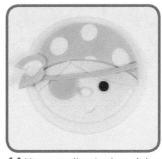

44 Use a scallop tool or piping nozzle edge to create a cute expression.

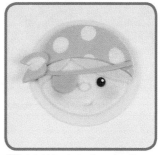

45 Add blush to the cheeks with petal dust and a little white edible paint to the eye.

46 Finally, personalise a cupcake disc with the child's name...in a pirate theme, of course!

Materials

Modelling paste:
White
Black
Red
Baking parchment
Edible glue

Tools

Craft knife/scalpel
Veining tool
Small, round cutters
Alphabet/number cutters

1 Trace the Skull template (thick black lines) from the rear of the book, using greaseproof paper or baking parchment.

2 Roll a thin layer of black paste and cut a circle – same size as your cake - from it using a cake board or plate as a template.

3 Roll a thin layer of white paste, lay the template on top and mark the outline of the skull part using a veining tool.

4 Following the indented outline created by your veining tool, use a sharp scalpel tool to cut the shape.

5 If you're not too confident cutting the eye/nose pieces from black paste then you can simply colour them with a black edible pen.

6 Repeat Steps 3 & 4 for the chin/mouth piece. If you want your skull to be less smiley, follow the broken line across the mouth area.

7 Repeat Steps 3 & 4 for the crossbones.

8 To add a bandana, roll a thin piece of red paste and lay the template on top, marking the outline at top of the skull and the broken lines for the remainder.

9 Attach this to your topper and add small white dots, if you wish.

10 If you like to add an eye patch, cut the shape on the template together with a long thin strip of black paste.

11 Arrange across your skull design.

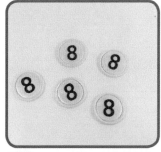

12 You can add coins with the child's age. Cut little discs, indent with a smaller cutter to create a rim and paint gold. Add the number in black.

13 You can add child's name to the topper by arranging the pieces differently. Lay the skull on top of the crossbones...

14 ...and add the child's name – simple!

Pirate Cake

Materials

Modelling paste:
White, Red
Black, Flesh
Yellow, Orange
Light & Dark Brown
Round covered cake
Baking parchment
Edible pen: black
Lustre dust: gold
Edible glue

Tools

Craft knife/scalpel
Paintbrush
Veining tool
Ball tool
No3 piping nozzle
Mini palette knife
Ribbon cutter
Cake smoother
Foam sponge for support
Pizza wheel

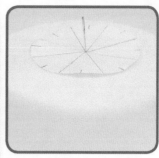

1 For a guide to placing the stripes on your cake, cut a round template, fold in half again and again to create 12 creases. Transfer lines onto the cake using a ruler.

2 Roll red and blue paste thinly then use the ribbon cutter to cut out strips approximately 1cm ($^1/_3$") wide.

3 Place the strips on the previously marked lines, gluing carefully, to create an even pattern. Trim the strips at centre and base.

4 Roll two long sausages of brown paste. Twist together to create rope effect. Wrap around the base of the cake and trim excess.

5 Roll white paste into two short sausage shapes for the legs of the pirate, cutting the ends to neaten.

6 For the leg stripes, roll black paste thinly and cut narrow stripes. Glue in place on legs.

7 Add two brown ovals for shoes.

8 Shape red paste into an oval, then flatten one end for the body. Thin the body slightly front to back.

9 Roll a rectangle of black paste and cut each end at an angle. Wrap and glue waistcoat in place.

10 Roll and flatten tiny yellow balls for buttons. Attach to the waistcoat using edible glue.

11 Roll two sausage shapes for the arms, cutting at each end to neaten. Attach to the body using edible glue.

12 Shape the hands from two pinches of flesh paste, adding finger details with veining tool. Glue in place.

13 Roll a ball of flesh paste for the head. Add the mouth with the end of the piping nozzle and black edible pen.

14 Roll and indent small balls for nose and ears as show. Glue in place, and draw one eye using edible black pen.

15 Shape the eye patch from a thin strip and cropped circle of black paste. Glue in place.

16 Roll into small ovals for hair then texture with the veining tool. Glue to head.

17 Roll an oval of red paste for the bandana, moulding it to the shape of the head and gluing in place.

18 Roll two teardrops and attach to the side of the cap using edible glue. Roll a ball for the knot and place over the join.

19 Form this shape for your parrot, using the veining tool to texture the tail feathers.

20 Now shape two wings. Start with a teardrop, flatten and texture as before. Attach with edible glue.

21 Shape the beak from a pinch of modelling paste. For the eyes roll two white balls and two smaller black balls.

22 Attach the beak and eyes to the head of the parrot using edible glue.

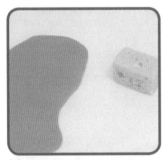

23 Make the treasure chest by either covering a small piece of cake in brown paste, or forming the whole shape from paste.

24 Texture the sides of the treasure chest to create a wooden effect.

25 Cut two straps and indent holes straps using the pointed end of the veining tool. Glue to the sides of the chest.

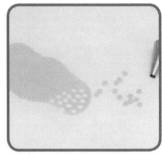

26 Cut out lots of little coins for the chest using a piping nozzle.

27 Stack the coins on the chest, gluing as you go. Add gold lustre dust if you have it.

28 Shape a lid for your treasure chest, using veining too to add the wooden effect.

29 Make straps for the lid as before. Attach to the lid with edible glue.

30 Position the lid of the treasure chest onto the body of the chest, perching it on the coins and secure in place with edible glue.

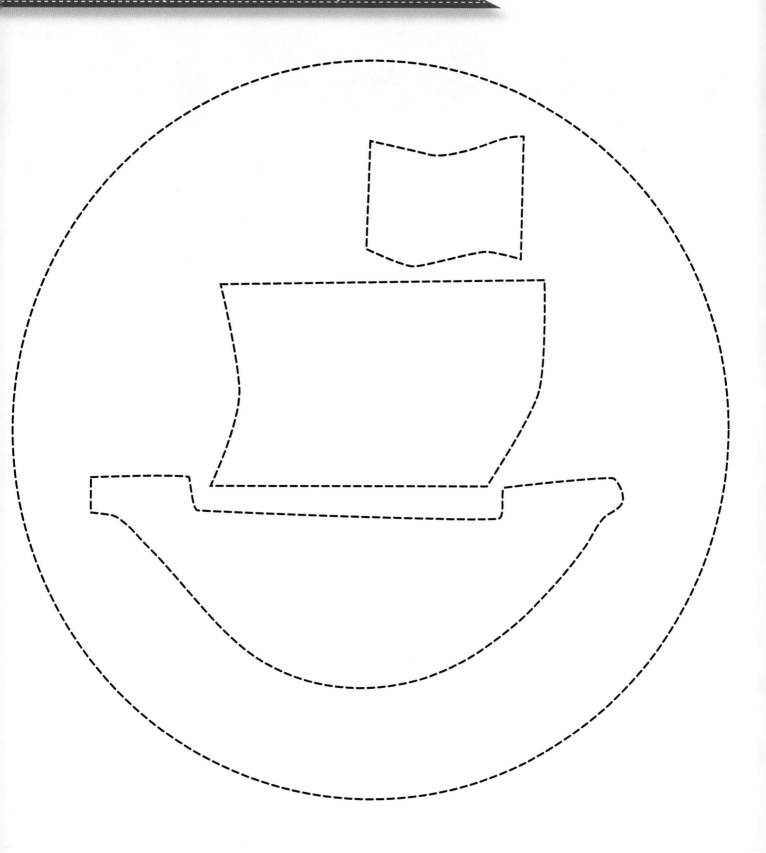

RECIPES ♥ TUTORIALS

RESOURCES ♥ INSPIRATION

The Cute & Easy Cake Toppers Collection is a fantastic range of mini tutorial books covering a wide range of party themes!

Oh Baby!
Cute & Easy Cake Toppers for any Baby Shower, Christening, Birthday or Baby Celebration!

Princesses, Fairies & Ballerinas!
Cute & Easy Cake Toppers for any Princess Party or Girly Celebration!

Puppies and Kittens & Pets, Oh My!
Puppies, Kittens, Bunnies, Pets and more!

Tiny Tea Parties!
Mini Food and Tiny Tea Parties That Look Good Enough To Eat!

Passion for Fashion!
Cute & Easy Cake Toppers! Shoes, Bags, Make-up and more! Mini Fashions That Look good Enough To Eat!

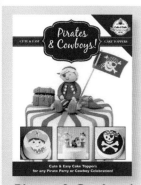

Pirates & Cowboys!
Cute & Easy Cake Toppers for any Pirate Party or Cowboy Celebration!

Cute and Easy Cake Toppers
Brenda Walton from Sugar High shows how to make cute and easy cake topper characters at home!

PLUS:

In The Jungle!
Roar, roar! Jungle animals galore!

Down On The Farm!
Tractors and farm animal fun!

Circus Time!
All The Fun Of The Big Top!

Vroom Vroom!
Trains, Planes, Cars, Diggers & more!

Love, Love, Love!
The loveliest toppers ever!

Over The Rainbow!
A world of rainbow fun!

Xmas Time!
Cute & Easy Xmas Cake Toppers!

and more!

Available in Paperback or instant PDF!

All books are available on Paperback : £6.95 / $10.95
Also available on instant PDF for just £2.95 / $5.95 from: www.cakeandbakeacademy.com

Search on Amazon under 'Cake & Bake Academy' or visit:
www.cakeandbakeacademy.com

Printed in Great Britain
by Amazon.co.uk, Ltd.,
Marston Gate.